Brighter Days Ahead

DEMETRIS CURRY

Photographer: Michael Moorer
Cover Design/Branding/Marketing/PR: inMMGroup, LLC
Publishing Services: Pen Legacy, LLC
Editing and Formatting: Carla M. Dean, U Can Mark My Word
Book Services: Writers Concierge

Library of Congress Cataloguing – in- Publication Data has been applied for.

ISBN: 979-8-9862796-2-6

PRINTED IN THE UNITED STATES OF AMERICA.
First Edition

Dedication

Between your cuts, bruises, pain, smiles, and laughter,

you produced little ol' me.

I am forever grateful.

Thank you so much, Mom.

Foreword

Bright: giving out or reflecting a lot of light; shining, radiating, luminous.

What if the brighter days you dreamed about, talked about, or even cried over are waiting on you? Festering inside you and tugging on you to release it. After denying the truth of who I was created to be and allowing certain seasons in my life to talk me out of the truth of God's light for so many years, it took everything within me to dig up God's light and place the reflection back on me. We all have the light of God in us, but we don't all acknowledge it. There are two discoveries that must take place in this process:

- You must believe there is a light, and you are the light.
- You must respond to the essence of what the light can do.

I defined the word "bright" above, and one of the keywords was "reflection." There will never be a brighter day for us if we don't see ourselves as a reflection of a brighter day. If you only evaluate yourself based on what you went through—instead of who you are—you will struggle with the reflection you were born with. The phenomenal Demetris Curry laid out a detailed blueprint to help you start on your pursuit of your Brighter Days Ahead. See, this is not just a title but a declaration over your life. Say it with me: "My brighter days are ahead of me. My brighter days are within me." Understand that whatever you say is what you will see. Whatever you say is what you will do.

Are you ready for your BRIGHTER DAY? Are you prepared to put in the work for your BRIGHTER DAY? Do you believe there's a BRIGHTER DAY for YOU? There's no day like the present to stop dreaming and even crying over what you want. Today is the day you are reminded to believe and start doing whatever it takes for you to see the reflection of God's light in you. Demetris told us that we must be persistent in our fight to see the light. She also said, "It will be a journey, not a race."

Demetris, thank you for your transparency and well-executed blueprint for us to follow. This book was straight to the point with steps to get us to our Brighter Days Ahead.

Michelle Washington

Editor-in-Chief of *Women of More Magazine*

Table of Contents

Brighter Days Ahead

Introduction

We have all been through some hard moments, right? So, where do we begin to draw the line? At what point do we decide to take back our lives? These are the questions I asked myself many years ago.

As a child, I learned to express myself through my love for arts via singing, interpretive dancing, and writing poems. At the age of sixteen, I was trying to figure out my role in this journey called life, as bullying and violence around me made me question my identity. One poem I wrote was titled "The Mood of Air." For the first time, I am sharing this poem with you as a reflection of how we can evolve further than our current situations.

Brighter Days Ahead was created to help others move in that direction by shifting our perception of what hard times are about and how that moment makes us stronger and wiser. We will visit well-known quotes throughout history that were instrumental, to say the least, in helping me create actions toward change. Use the

Reflection pages to share your current thoughts on how you can implement your change.

Let us begin!

The Mood of Air

In the creation of time comes a spark of light
Ongoing challenges of despair highlighted with
crevices of joy

Yet, the sound doesn't stop there...
Movement of flexibility glides, giving freshness &
breezes of unthinkable wonder.

Hills and mountains of landscaped brilliance topped
with frosting of whitened dew,
bringing delight to the eye.

Calmness, solitude, and metaphoric tides flow near,
delegating the theory of motion.

Energy forceful yet fragile—holding the patience of
nature close while abiding the laws of realism as the
day comes forth.

~ Demetris Curry

"Out of suffering have emerged
the strongest souls; the most massive
characters are seared
with scars."

– Khalil Gibran (Ka-lil Je-bran)
(1883-1931)

From Gunpoint to Strength

This quote by Khalil Gibran was my point of rescue in a time of my life when I was confronting hardship, suffering, and sacrificing. When I was a bank teller, I survived one of the most horrific bank robberies in banking history, according to law enforcement. The robbers held up our teller line with live ammunition, shoved us aggressively, and held a shotgun to my head. I had never been more scared in my life than at that moment. As I tried not to look at him directly, I could not avoid noticing that his eyes looked young. It later made me think hard about some of our youth's choices and the lives they affect thereafter. They were quickly apprehended miles from the bank, and as if that day were not hard enough, the court subpoenaed each person to testify.

As I relived this crime every day for months, I had trouble sleeping, was scared to stay in my home, and constantly looked over my shoulders. Eventually, I resigned from my job. I couldn't muster the courage to walk back into that bank. I even let my college courses go with incomplete grades, an act that didn't reflect the standards of the honor student I was. It was an emotional scar that followed me for years. But I can tell you today that it made me stronger and sharpened my senses of my surroundings.

So, as we look again at the quote, "The most massive characters are seared with scars," think not that your scar is too great. Emerging is greatness! What have your darkest moments taught you? Did that chapter of your life make you change? What are you doing about it?

Reflection

_____

_____

_____

_____

_____

_____

_____

_____

_____

_____

_____

_____

_____

Demetris Curry

Brighter Days Ahead

_____

_____

_____

_____

_____

_____

_____

_____

_____

_____

_____

_____

_____

"Start by doing what's necessary, then what's possible; and suddenly you are doing the impossible."

– Saint Francis of Assis
(1181-1286)

Shoot for the Impossible

*E*very dynasty has its stages; you must remember this when building a legacy. This is crucial to learn. At times, I had to take undesirable positions in a company only to get my foot in the door (and pay the bills). Have you ever been in this position?

I have worked in factories with no central air conditioning in the summer or heat in the winter. I cut lawns between paychecks as a side job to make ends meet, and I even cleaned houses part-time after leaving my full-time job to bring in a little extra income. It was my SURVIVAL season! We do what is necessary to survive while bearing in mind that the SEASON is only temporary. As you continue to evolve and learn trades that genuinely interest you, you'll learn new things.

Educate yourself on what you have always wanted to do but never had the chance to. Working on self-development is crucial in establishing a "setup" that will ONE DAY support what YOU once thought was IMPOSSIBLE! Think of the great leaders today who started off working in various jobs they hated but eventually got to where they wanted with time and consistency. Their survival move developed into a major shift—not only in their career but also in the amount of income they earned. This is where many are today!

How do you manifest a major move in your life? Have you thought about where you want to be and started gaining the expertise that will get you there?

Reflection

_____

_____

_____

_____

_____

_____

_____

_____

_____

_____

_____

_____

Brighter Days Ahead

"Success is a journey, not a destination. The doing is usually more important than the outcome."

– Arthur Ashe Jr. (1943-1993)

The Success Destination

*I*f Rome wasn't built in a day, why would we think our journey or vision must manifest in a day? I am a perfectionist at heart, but I also remind myself daily that some things take time to manifest. In making the journey, I realize life is just that…A JOURNEY!

Have you ever taken a road trip from state to state and wanted to hurry up and reach your resort or hotel? Years ago, while driving thirteen hours to Miami, something suddenly hit me. A soothing voice in my head murmured the words: *Don't forget to enjoy the view.* I had an epiphany that the journey was just as important as the destination and tried to take in the scenery between points A and B. There is much to learn in the interim of getting to a new location. The landmarks, terrain, climate, and even the time it takes to get to the next location all play a part in the journey.

If I close my eyes to the lessons learned from one location to another, it's easy to miss the big picture! I had to train myself to take the first step in creating consistency towards a goal. There will be some good days and some bad days, yet even when the terrain seems rough, we can keep building our momentum as time progresses. In the interim of the journey we learn much about ourselves.

Have you taken in the lessons you've learned from location to location or season to season? What key lessons made an impact on this trip to success? Did you find better ways to achieve a given goal you never expected would unfold? What would you do differently on the next journey?

Reflection

_____

_____

_____

_____

_____

_____

_____

_____

_____

_____

_____

_____

Brighter Days Ahead

_____

_____

_____

_____

_____

_____

_____

_____

_____

_____

_____

_____

_____

"Whatever the mind can conceive and believe, it can achieve."

– Napoleon Hill (1883-1970)

Conceive, Believe, Achieve

*N*apoleon Hill hit the nail on the head with this message. I hold this quote as a mantra because it embodies all I am working to achieve. Even when people say, "That's impossible," my response is always, "Your limitations are not my own."

There was a time when I believed good things weren't meant to happen to me—the gifts of life were only reserved for other people. I erroneously thought having a better life was simply not in the cards for me. Where did that limiting belief come from? And how do I get past it? The shift came once I renovated my mindset and accepted that I deserved all the good things life had to offer.

Something I learned the hard way: *If you don't know your own worth, someone else will certainly tell you what they think your worth is.* That includes your attributes or lack thereof. Once you truly realize what you can do, the limited mindset of others becomes less important to you. Belief is where it all begins. Where is your belief?

Can your mind conceive being debt-free? Can you imagine not living from paycheck to paycheck, or have you conditioned yourself to ACCEPT lack in your life? Think about it! Do you allow people who place limits on their lives to influence what you believe?

Reflection

_____

_____

_____

_____

_____

_____

_____

_____

_____

_____

_____

_____

Brighter Days Ahead

"If you care at all, you'll get some results. If you care enough, you'll get incredible results."

– Jim Rohn
(1930-2009)

Do You Care?

espite what the goal is, everyone is driven by their own WHY. How important this WHY is to you will dictate how much time you spend fighting to meet the objective or educating yourself on it. If you care a lot and the WHY is big enough, your outcome will be even greater!

When I worked in corporate America, much of my time went into working long hours away from my family, getting just enough time at home on weekends to sleep and start over again. It wasn't until our son started needing more of my time for sports and school assignments that I realized re-working my schedule wasn't negotiable. It had to be done, and my family was a big enough reason for why. The tasks pushed those important things in my life to the back burner. So, I created a plan to start moving into the entrepreneurial space where I was still helping the community build a solid financial future while allowing myself the opportunity to do it in a different capacity. It was not easy!

There was a lot of trial and error and many sleepless nights mind-mapping plans of action and learning more about myself to move in the direction that would be most impactful.

So, ask yourself this: How big is your WHY? Why do you want this job? What do you plan to do with the money from it? If you're working to send your child to a private school, why is it important for them to go to that school? Break down your WHY into the smallest morsels and see if it really is your WHY.

Reflection

_____

_____

_____

_____

_____

_____

_____

_____

_____

_____

_____

_____

Brighter Days Ahead

_____

_____

_____

_____

_____

_____

_____

_____

_____

_____

_____

_____

_____

_____

"Give, and it will be given to you:
good measure, pressed down, shaken
together, and running over will be put
into your bosom. For the same
measure that you use, it will be
measured back to you."

– Luke 6:38 (NKJV)

Keep Going!

This message has carried me in so many ways. Knowing that we are blessed by our good deeds that follow us for all the days of our lives has given me strength. The message brings me back to a dream in 2006 that remains etched in my memory today:

A brown cardboard box perched upon a white kitchen countertop. The box was overflowing with balls of cash growing in volume and snapping from the bottom of the box like the old popcorn poppers. The balls of dollars started falling out of the box, and a set of hands grabbed handfuls of the cash out of the box and threw it on the counter, where other hands picked it up. Yet the money flowing out of the box seemed limitless and never-ending. No matter how many times the hands grabbed money from the top, it kept flowing!

This message behind the dream was overflow. Because of my

nurturing spirit, I tended to give myself to others who needed it most. The dream was a valuable lesson in giving—of how those deeds will follow you and bestow your life with overflow beyond what most of us ever dreamed imaginable. Whether it be the giving of your time, services, lending a listening ear, or even providing some sound advice that could help someone, the return could be more than you ever dreamed possible. How powerful is that?

Have you considered that being a blessing can align you to a greater good? What can you give to someone that can change their lives?

Reflection

_____

_____

_____

_____

_____

_____

_____

_____

_____

_____

_____

_____

Brighter Days Ahead

"That which we persist in doing becomes easier, not that the task itself has become easier, but that our ability to perform it has improved."

– Ralph Waldo Emerson
(1803-1882)

Be Persistent in Your Fight

I think back to high school when I was enrolled in performing arts for classical voice and interpretive dance. I loved both, but the rehearsals, recitals, competitions, and showcases were tiresome. Singing for so long would create painful sore throats, and I experienced sprains and pulled muscles during dancing. Some routines seemed outside my range of capability and required more of myself to master.

Despite how I felt at that time and how tired I was some days, my appreciation for the craft never wavered. My love of the arts gave me the strength to continue from one competition to the next. I learned to be persistent in mastering routines—pushing my body to the limit and training my mind to never falter or give up.

Music and the arts taught me a valuable lesson in preparing and perfecting a seamless performance. I constantly asked myself:

Am I giving it my all? Is this the best I can do, or is there room for improvement? Performing also gave me an outlet to find what I enjoyed despite other hardships that stole from the joy and excitement.

How about you? Are you being persistent in achieving what you desire? Does it call for constant practice or repetition? Have you held yourself accountable through the pain and uneasy feelings? What are YOU doing to master your gift?

Reflection

_____

_____

_____

_____

_____

_____

_____

_____

_____

_____

_____

Brighter Days Ahead

"Most of the important things in the world have been accomplished by people who have kept on trying when there seemed to be no hope at all."

– Dale Carnegie
(1888-1955)

Where is Your Faith in You?

*A*s a teenager, I remember my mom becoming a single mother to her two children. It was new territory for her, being the sole provider of the household. As she worked two jobs and attended night school in hopes of getting a degree, I had to learn how to take care of my brother. I was assigned the chores of cooking, cleaning, ironing, and homework while she worked hard to provide.

It seemed impossible for a young mother to juggle multiple jobs, attend a technical college, and raise two young children simultaneously. But my mom stayed hopeful and literally cried her way through some days to make it. After many years of juggling, she obtained her degree in cosmetology. Where did she find the energy?

As a teenager, my responsibilities of helping around the house were part of daily life. I learned how to run a home as a kid. It was tough, but it prepared me to run my own home one day. We made many sacrifices as a family, and I remember thinking as a child that life was hard. I thought to myself: *Is this what adulthood will be for me, too? Will I be able to handle it?* Those were the questions I was most concerned with then. The answers to those questions could be found in my mom, and they gave me the motivation to become who I am today.

Though being a single parent is common nowadays, we often fail to realize they are the cornerstone of our society. Our society is built by people performing these duties every day and taking on roles in the household to provide for their families and prepare them for a better future. This message from Dale Carnegie teaches us that all the important things we see parents do today are carving the way to a brighter future for themselves and their children.

What is your motivation to do something important in your lifetime? Is there a part of you that has a desire to make a change in your family, community, and even the world? What does that look like in your eyes? What do you hope to accomplish for the betterment of yourself and others you love?

Reflection

_____

_____

_____

_____

_____

_____

_____

_____

_____

_____

_____

Brighter Days Ahead

"Faith is taking the first step,
even when you don't see the
whole staircase."

Martin Luther King, Jr.
(1929-1968)

The Art of Giving

It took me a long time to truly understand the importance of faith. Only through time and experience did I come to realize what faith meant to me. Strong faith is what carried me through many obstacles, and it's a brave leap to make because it's about believing in something that isn't concrete or present.

When I first relied on faith to build my brand, I was terrified. I had always been the person behind the scenes in my career, making my bosses look good. Yes, I said it! I took pride in making my boss look good because I enjoyed what I did—helping others achieve their dreams. So, naturally, when I walked out of corporate America many years ago, confessing that I doubted myself would be an understatement. I did not want to do it. I kept searching for reasons to avoid being the center of attention; I turned down countless opportunities presented to me, sometimes avoiding the conversation altogether.

I needed faith of the size of a mustard seed, and that's literally all I had—a tiny mustard seed of faith and my innate gift of helping others build success. It was time to use that gift on myself. I had no idea if it would work. I bet against myself on numerous occasions, and because of that, I had to create a circle of accountability that believed in me more than I did. Building a business requires daily work. Each day I wake up, I must continue to hold myself accountable to "me" and no one else.

Do you have faith in yourself? Where is your faith in your dreams, your purpose, and your destiny? Are you speaking your truth into your life? If not, get a journal and write down your thoughts, dreams, and desires today! Then decide on a timeframe and do at least one thing daily to get closer to your goal.

Reflection

_____

_____

_____

_____

_____

_____

_____

_____

_____

_____

_____

Brighter Days Ahead

_____

_____

_____

_____

_____

_____

_____

_____

_____

_____

_____

_____

_____

"Let all bitterness, and wrath, and anger, and clamour, and evil speaking, be put away from you, with all malice: And be ye kind one to another, tenderhearted, forgiving one another, even as God for Christ's sake hath forgiven you."

– Ephesians 4:31-32 (KJV)

Learn to Forgive

When someone has hurt you, forgiving can certainly be a process. Yes, forgiveness is a POWER that only you bestow. This was an area I struggled with immensely. It took me a long time to realize the anger I was so fervently holding onto was a double-edged sword—and the edge shaping me was much sharper. My heart was filled to the brim with bitterness.

Have you ever had relationships that turned out to be completely different than what you made them out to be in your head? I have been there. I struggled to walk away sometimes, but the pain of staying grew greater than the pain of letting go. And I had to walk away from those that inflicted harm—intentional or unintentional. Clinging to toxic friendships and relationships only brought turmoil into other areas of my life and ultimately made the act of forgiveness more difficult to execute. No matter how desirable a bond felt superficially, I learned to forgive and move on to find out what life had in store for me.

If I had chosen to hold on to the pain and anger rather than heal and grow, I would have blocked my blessings. Unforgiveness is sabotage to GREATNESS, and though it may take time to heal, your path will become clearer as you take control and learn to let go of those things holding you back from happier days.

What are you holding on to that you know you need to let go of? Is holding on to that anger or pain working to your advantage right now? How can you use it to move closer to your purpose?

Reflection

_____

_____

_____

_____

_____

_____

_____

_____

_____

_____

_____

_____

Demetris Curry

_____

_____

_____

_____

_____

_____

_____

_____

_____

_____

_____

_____

_____

_____

_____

Brighter Days Ahead

"Courage is about doing what you're afraid to do. There can be no courage unless you're scared."

– Eddie Rickenbacker
(1890-1973)

The Courage Vehicle

As a business owner, it took courage to believe in my ability to count on myself. When I first started many years ago, I was nervous and scared out of my mind. What was I afraid of? I was afraid of SUCCESS!

Most people would say, "I'm afraid to fail. I'm afraid I will not do well at it." Yet no one is born into this world with a talent that doesn't require months or years of practice and repetition. I may have committed huge mistakes when starting my business, but I learned how to build networks and relationships and taught myself how to use other people's mistakes as lessons to live by.

As I grew wiser and observed the habits and routines of other successful people, I learned that failure propelled them to the next level. Abraham Lincoln, amongst many others, was renowned for what he accomplished. Yet, no one mentions how many times he had to fail in order to succeed. People always mention that Thomas Edison invented the light bulb, but they never start with the fact that he made a thousand unsuccessful attempts beforehand. You MUST travel down "Failure Avenue" to reach "Success Boulevard," and your vehicle shall be Courage. No matter how bad the traffic, keep moving inch by inch! Each inch counts, and if you think you cannot make it, you have already directed your path.

I challenge you to get in the COURAGE automobile and drive down "Failure Avenue" to reach "Success Boulevard!"

Reflection

_____

_____

_____

_____

_____

_____

_____

_____

_____

_____

_____

_____

Brighter Days Ahead

"People create their own questions because they are afraid to look straight. All you have to do is look straight and see the road, and when you see it, don't sit looking at it—walk."

– Ayn Rand
(1905-1982)

Self-Doubt

This message is phenomenal, for we all have done this. We question our ability to do what we set out to do. Many of us are probably even doing that as we speak! I started this project of writing *Brighter Days Ahead* in 2012, and it took years for me to release it. Why? I was full of self-doubt. I wasn't confident enough in my ability to be an author! I wondered if I had it in me to share my story and still be accepted by my peers—to tell the world that I am far from perfect; I have flaws and have made more mistakes than I could count. However, there is more to me than meets the eye—there is more to my story than what I post on business profiles and social media. I silenced the imposter in me and finally asked myself: *Can I do this?* How many of us have looked at a step-by-step guide to fulfilling a task and ended up lazing away without ever taking the first step?

How powerful is it to say, "I want to be at a certain place in my life," but then you r-e-f-u-s-e to do the work or walk towards the vision! Keep your eyes straight ahead on the task at hand. Travel the road to reach your destination, for standing in one spot will never GET—YOU—THERE! I promise you.

I challenge you to question yourself less on what could go WRONG and meditate more on what could go RIGHT. I have decided to walk forward in my purpose and my dream. Ask yourself: *Am I walking ahead, or am I standing still? What is holding me back?* Think about it, write it down, and attack it!

Reflection

_____

_____

_____

_____

_____

_____

_____

_____

_____

_____

_____

_____

_____

Brighter Days Ahead

_____

_____

_____

_____

_____

_____

_____

_____

_____

_____

_____

_____

_____

"You see things; and you say 'Why?'
But I dream things that never were;
and I say, 'Why not?'"

– George Bernard Shaw
(1856-1950)

And Why Not?

I absolutely love this message because it defines my general attitude after all my personal growth. When I came to the realization that all the inventions we have around us—from computers to traffic lights and automobiles—someone had to say, "I don't see why that wouldn't be possible." Let's stop right there and think about that. Yes, it is possible. Why? Because someone believed it was.

It is possible to communicate on a boxed system through networks and IP connectivity from city to city, country to country, and even in space as astronauts communicate back to Earth. Yes, it's even possible to have machines picking cotton fields that once required hours of manual labor by delicate farm hands. I bet our ancestors did not even imagine machines would be plowing the land they once worked from sun-up to sun-down, blistering in pain. My family history is rooted in working in the fields picking fruit and vegetables since the family business provided for the family.

Dynasties have been built from the inventions of those who went against the grain, against those naysayers who asked why they were even attempting such a thing. A key component to know: it's not their vision. It's yours! All these inventions were once DREAMS, ladies and gentlemen.

What is the difference between their dreams and yours? There's only one thing you must do; KEEP AT IT UNTIL IT FLOURISHES!

Reflection

_____

_____

_____

_____

_____

_____

_____

_____

_____

_____

_____

_____

Brighter Days Ahead

_____

_____

_____

_____

_____

_____

_____

_____

_____

_____

_____

_____

_____

"You were meant to be here.
This is your time."

– Herbert "Herb" P. Brooks, Jr.
(1937-2003)

You Have Purpose

W ow, what confirmation! Each of us should adopt the belief that we were put here in this body and on these lands for a purpose. I can tell you that it was easy for me to doubt my purpose, especially after many years of battling crippling self-doubt, low self-esteem, and a deep-seated belief that I did not deserve to have more than enough, let alone an overflow of abundance.

Part of the quote that says, "You are meant to be here," puts me in the space of self-acceptance and understanding that my presence on this earth is by no means a mistake, for I have a purpose. We all do! What is tragic is we tend to get lost in all the other frivolous elements of life as we try to figure out who we are supposed to be instead of attempting to embody our life's purpose.

I remember my years in college, during which I tried to figure out my next move in life and the career I should pursue. I thought college would teach me that; instead, it showed me where I did not want to go. That was even more important. I started off in majors I admired but had no passion for and essentially decided to let go of academic majors that were not making me happy.

When I read, *"This is your time,"* I took it to heart and leaned on finding my purpose. Let's figure out your purpose today. When moving from one level to another, we must saturate our minds and thoughts with this message—a short message with a huge impact!

Reflection

_____

_____

_____

_____

_____

_____

_____

_____

_____

_____

_____

Brighter Days Ahead

"Opportunity is missed by most people because it is dressed in overalls and looks like work."

– Thomas Edison
(1847-1931)

Put Your Overalls On

I'm sure we have all missed great opportunities because of being afraid to push up our sleeves and work for them. I remember when we set our minds on buying our first home. We had no idea what it would take to get approved for financing as a young couple.

Still early in my career, it was our first time going through the process of getting pre-approval and setting ourselves up to do so. From working extra hours, cutting back spending in a major way, saving every dime we could get our hands on for a down payment, and paying down credit cards to get our scores higher and secure a better interest rate. It was months of preparation and back-and-forth conversations with loan officers to achieve the goal.

Nothing is given to you on a silver platter without having to nurture it and make sure it grows to the point of success. This message was my wake-up call because it made me realize I was the only one accountable for my success. I knew nothing worthwhile came easily, and I would have to sweat to get what I wanted—in marriage and business.

If you've ever heard the quote "Anything worth having is worth working for," it is beyond true. No matter how many times I must crawl through the trenches or push through an uphill battle to get there, I will get it done! Will YOU have the same grit to do the same in your life?

Reflection

_____

_____

_____

_____

_____

_____

_____

_____

_____

_____

_____

_____

Brighter Days Ahead

_____

_____

_____

_____

_____

_____

_____

_____

_____

_____

_____

_____

"You can do anything if you have enthusiasm. Enthusiasm is the yeast that makes your hopes rise to the stars. With it, there is accomplishment. Without it, there are only alibis."

– Henry Ford
(1863-1947)

What's Your Turning Point?

*H*ave you ever heard of anyone reaching the top without being excited about what they were doing? ABSOLUTELY NOT! When people say, "Demetris, you're always smiling. You're always excited," they do not truly know my story. See, there is a story behind every smile. Would you believe I have seen some very dark days in my life? I was not even sure I would make it this far. Even though I carry excitement within me, I know that enthusiasm is the diesel of dreams. I know that hopes by themselves without positive energy mean nothing! I also know that without helping others see the light in their lives, the light in yours will flicker farther away.

How can I be a light to others as their coach, agent, consultant, motivator, etc., if I am gloomy, pacing in despair, frowning all the time, and walking around like life is over? It is that bright light of excitement shining at the edges of your goal that makes the achievement even sweeter.

I dare you to get some excitement in your belly for what you are striving to achieve—to press to the limit any negative thought that once held you back from achieving greatness!

Reflection

_____

_____

_____

_____

_____

_____

_____

_____

_____

_____

_____

Brighter Days Ahead

"The turning point in the process of growing up is when you discover the core of strength within you that survives all hurt."

– Max Lerner
(1902-1992)

Use That Fear to Build

*I*t's okay to get up when you have fallen. It's okay to start over. "Fall down seven times, stand up eight," as the saying goes. When I was one of the top retail sales representatives in my field, I worked long hours and sometimes even took work home with me, hustling my weekends away due to the shortage of staff and growing workload. Nonetheless, I put in an easy 60-65 hours a week and was on salary, occasionally receiving bonuses in volume. Because of that, I was often highlighted in the quarter newsletter for sales. Always in the top 3 for all company locations!

That being said, I had a shocking moment when my husband's new job required relocation. I requested a letter of recommendation since all the top executives knew me by name and gave me leads to handle when available. After two weeks of asking, I was denied a letter of recommendation from an executive who often called upon me for his elite clients. His message was, "Demetris, we love you here, and if you ever want to come back, our doors are always open. However, if I give you a letter of recommendation, I would have to give one to everyone else." What a BLOW!

I felt defeated and unappreciated. I instantly thought about all the times I sacrificed time with my family and all the extra feats I did that were not part of my job description. What did I do with this lesson? I did all I could do! I got up and prepared to relocate with my husband, hoping to find another job without that letter of recommendation. Though it took months, I had to start over within my career as a temporary employee without ever finding a permanent position. While the wind had been knocked out of me, I eventually opened my own home-based business. I learned to have a plan B always and never let ANYONE have total dominion over my destiny.

Is there a situation that knocked you down, and you got back up? Think about it. You made it through. You are a champion because you got back up!

Reflection

_____

_____

_____

_____

_____

_____

_____

_____

_____

_____

_____

_____

Brighter Days Ahead

_____

_____

_____

_____

_____

_____

_____

_____

_____

_____

_____

_____

_____

"Most of our obstacles would melt away if, instead of cowering before them, we should make up our minds to walk boldly through them."

– Orison Swett Marden
(1850-1924)

Acceptance Is Key

When I look back to when I first walked away from working for others, the fear was beyond explanation. I dreaded being out on my own and not having the sturdy structure of the corporate environment to fall back on. I was unsure of myself. I was led to believe I was inferior to my counterparts. People who are afraid of your shine can do some ugly, hateful things to make you feel worthless.

For years, all the knowledge I learned was etched into my mind, and once you learn something, you can't unlearn it. You never know how your past will open doors to your future. So, I tapped into that. I learned much in banking, such as how to use finance projects with the right leverage. What I did not know is that those key elements of finance would one day allow me to look out for families and even teach it in communities.

Of course, I still get butterflies on new projects, but what once scared me to death now excites me more than ever. All I needed was the strength to face it. Achieve that goal and keep pressing forward.

Reflection

_____

_____

_____

_____

_____

_____

_____

_____

_____

_____

_____

_____

Brighter Days Ahead

"Self-acceptance comes from meeting life's challenges vigorously. Don't numb yourself to your trials and difficulties, nor build mental walls to exclude pain from your life. You will find peace not by trying to escape your problems, but by confronting them courageously. You will find peace not in denial, but in victory."

– Swami Sivananda (Se-va-non-do)
(1887-1963)

Map the Course

Self-acceptance was never easy for me. I always found myself yearning for something else—I wished I looked like other girls; I envied healthy relationships and friendships; I wondered if other people in my life were also struggling with their identity. I was unsure who I was supposed to be because I was constantly trying to find my place in life. How does one switch that uncertainty? At what point does the heart shift to believe that you are worth having more? That you are worth pursuing the happiness you deserve. And we are not talking about the accumulation of materialistic things but the things that make you happy from within. Inner peace. The ability to have a restful season. An unbothered time of enjoying where you are in life.

There is a place within that starts to change your outlook of who you are, and when that piece of you rises, listen! What are you doing today to gain the happiness and self-worth that is rightfully yours? Are you ready to create options for a more enjoyable life? Why not? Finding peace and self-acceptance during a storm can feel unheard of. It can be agonizing to try and breathe through the pain. Yes, I know. If you asked me today what I learned through my difficult moments, I would say not to discount the challenges I've overcome.

That is why I allow myself to share with you how I have made it through so far…why I embrace these trials and tribulations and feel a deep sense of gratitude for how they molded me into who I am today. This is my personal journey; this is how I got here.

Reflection

_____

_____

_____

_____

_____

_____

_____

_____

_____

_____

_____

_____

Brighter Days Ahead

———————————————————————

———————————————————————

———————————————————————

———————————————————————

———————————————————————

———————————————————————

———————————————————————

———————————————————————

———————————————————————

———————————————————————

———————————————————————

———————————————————————

———————————————————————

———————————————————————

"Whatever course you decide upon, there is always someone to tell you that you are wrong. There are always difficulties arising, which tempt you to believe that your critics are right. To map out a course of action and follow it to an end requires courage."

– Ralph Waldo Emerson
(1803-1882)

The Push Through: Persevere

There will always be someone who will tell you who they *think* you are and what you can achieve. Expect it! Don't be surprised by it! If everyone could do what you do, they would be doing it! Some claim "that will never work" or "that's a waste of time"—even "you need to let that mess go!" What they are doing is putting limitations on what they believe you can do because they have placed limitations on what THEY can do. Understand this to the fullest because if you don't, that negative seed can disrupt your desire to step into your desired happiness.

I have experienced this many times in my life and had to make up my mind on my course of action. The question is: Who are you living for? Are you here to please someone else? Or are you trying to become the best version of yourself? And ultimately, is that person the type of person you want to have in the front row of your show? Have they achieved a morsel of where you are headed?

I have learned on many occasions that although you may have a certain amount of respect for those dear to you, sometimes they need to have a balcony view of where you are headed until they see it does mean a lot to you—after which they make the decision to move to the floor level of your life's theatre.

Your job is to be okay with allowing them to pick their seat; they can always upgrade accommodations later! And if they don't, that's their choice. Staying steadfast requires courage. Will you stand behind your own production?

Reflection

_____

_____

_____

_____

_____

_____

_____

_____

_____

_____

_____

_____

"I do not think there is any other quality so essential to success of any kind as the quality of perseverance. It overcomes almost everything, even nature."

– John D. Rockefeller, Sr.
(1839-1937)

Don't Quit on Yourself

W hat I am experiencing right now is the art of perseverance. It is a choice! Think back to what we have covered so far, for this quality is mandatory in carving out a sculpture of where you hope to be, despite where you came from. Most people get stuck in the pain of past hurts and disappointments. Maybe they expected more from a friendship or love, and when things did not pan out the way they planned, they felt lost, desperate, and depressed. We tend to think we cannot persevere through the hurt or pain. Yes, I have been there!

Where you come from in no way determines where you are going. But as easy as that is to say, we have the hardest time accepting this truth. We fall prey to what we have been told and what others have outlined us to be, giving no thought to our dreams and desires. Today, we call victory…we proclaim abundance…we declare prosperity for generations to come!

Who you once were is no more. You have shed the old you and become the new you.

What will you overcome today? What are you claiming right now that you will take control over and get to the other side of?

Reflection

_____

_____

_____

_____

_____

_____

_____

_____

_____

_____

_____

_____

Brighter Days Ahead

"Arise, awake,
and stop not until the goal is reached."

– Swami Vivekanando (Ve-ve-ka-nan-do)
(1863-1902)

Wake Up!

How many of you feel drained as you fight for your goal? Success is not an overnight endeavor. In the meantime, I have chosen to surround myself with people with the same mindset as me—that of abundance and perpetual growth.

Have you ever heard the saying, "If you hang around four broke people, you will likely be the fifth"? Well, it's a true statement. I like to call my circle the "Power of 5," where each person has a quality that may not be my strength. Iron sharpens iron every day of the week! Another trick is finding a pace that you can consistently work in without getting burned out. In most cases, your pace will be much different than that of others, but the trick is to make sure you set a realistic goal because it may take time to manifest. Be mindful not to hibernate while the world continues around you.

"Wake up" is what I tell myself when needed. There is still

work to be done. Does this sound like you? If so, your hibernation is over. Arise! Awake!

Reflection

_____

_____

_____

_____

_____

_____

_____

_____

_____

_____

_____

_____

_____

Brighter Days Ahead

_____

_____

_____

_____

_____

_____

_____

_____

_____

_____

_____

_____

_____

_____

"A champion is someone who gets up
when he can't."

– Jack Dempsey
(1895-1983)

You Are a Champion!

What better way to end this series than to declare the champion in YOU! If a champion is what they call it, I receive it today. Will you? I remember many years ago when my husband and I were a newly married couple. Both of us lived through job layoffs and literally lived in the "paycheck-to-paycheck" category, where eating canned sausages and peanut butter sandwiches for dinner was a must. We lived off one paycheck to pay two car notes, rent, credit cards, and student loans.

I became a professional bill juggler. Yes, I did! I'm laughing at myself as I type this because you have no idea. Every pay period (and whenever possible), I paid bills right before the delinquency date could hit the credit report, protecting our credit as much as possible. Nearly losing everything, we had to join a consumer counseling service for assistance in knocking down bill payments and saving us from forfeiting our assets as newlyweds.

We never asked for help or told anyone what we were going through. We pushed through by doing odd jobs to fill income gaps and cut our expenses in areas we could control, such as fast food, entertainment, and even paying others to cut and/or style our hair. Yes, there were days we never thought we could get back up, but we were a family that knew it was only temporary; we refused to let those days define our future. That was nearly twenty years ago, and we overcame that.

If you are feeling defeated, take my testimonies shared with you in this book and use them for yourself. You are NOT alone; we have all had dark days! Anyone who says they haven't is lying to you.

I WANT YOU TO GET INTO MOTION. GET UP! SPEAK UP! Did you know you had this kind of power within? Absolutely, you do! It is now your time to have everything you've worked so hard to achieve. No one is holding you back but you! Take the time to review your dreams, visions, and goals. Now that you have some guidance and have heard about some of my hardest days, learn from my mistakes and use them for your gain. I hope you feel inspired.

I believe in you!
Now it's time for you to believe in yourself!

Reflection

_____

_____

_____

_____

_____

_____

_____

_____

_____

_____

_____

Brighter Days Ahead

About the Author

D emetris "Dee" Curry serves her community as a published author, speaker, Insurance Wellness Strategist, and Commercial Real Estate Broker. With nearly twenty-five years of experience in banking/financial services, wealth accumulation and maintenance, bank auditing, analytical reasoning, life and disability insurance procurement, and asset building, Dee has a reputation for helping people optimize their risk portfolios while creating and maintaining the lifestyles they deem suitable for their financial health and well-being. Dee holds a formal degree in Business Administration with a concentration in Banking and Finance, is Real Estate Lending Certified, and licensed as a Life & Health and Fixed Annuities provider.

Known for exhibiting one-of-a-kind integrity in the field of insurance and finances and leading with a remarkable and rare passion to serve, Dee began to understand early in life the importance of financial security and the effects of the lack of protection preparation in families. After finding herself and other family members being left to delay personal and professional goals due to the unforeseen burden of financial responsibility resulting from the untimely demise of those who had not properly financially equipped their loved ones to live lives that were free of financial distress, Dee vowed to ensure that families around the globe become more cognizant of the tools and resources available for financial wealth and security.

Dee stands firm in her belief that one cannot truly live their "best life" without first having the peace in knowing that they have created a financial wealth space in which their children, their children's children, and their children can also experience wondrous magnitudes of financial freedom. Demetris is a well-respected and much sought-after advocate for generational financial health education and life insurance benefits literacy.

Dee is Founder, Chief Broker, and Wealth Strategist at Inspired for Greatness, LLC, who inspires individuals and business owners by using a comprehensive approach providing strategic techniques in advancing with intention. With the focus areas of life and business that are impactful to a more secure position, she aids in creating options towards improved business and personal goals, the implementation of generational wealth opportunities, and providing resources built to assist in further career aspirations. As a development and consulting firm, Inspired for Greatness, LLC serves individuals and organizations worldwide through wealth planning, insurance acquisition, and financial sustainability services. Responsible for driving profit growth and negotiating contracts for organization leaders, Dee's work with financial institutions has proved pivotal in helping to win multimillion and billion-dollar servicing bids. Encompassing the constructs of the Suitability Analysis Review (SAR) into her training, consulting, and education model, Demetris has developed a dynamic, customizable, evidence-based, and results-driven strategy to establish long-term familial wealth. Having emerged as a leading expert in her field, Dee's financial education and coaching programs prepare and position individuals and families to attract, attain, and sustain wealth for generations to come.

Author Features:

WBRC https://www.wbrc.com/video/2020/09/22/tips-gaining-financial-independence/

Black News https://blacknews.com/news/demetris-curry-5-ways-to-preventing-financial-child-abuse-in-african-american-families/

"Your Life the Remix" Talking Women Issues in Finance, Apple Podcast: https://podcasts.apple.com/us/podcast/your-life-the-remix/id1550477150?i=1000522348214

inCity Magazine
https://www.youtube.com/watch?v=3OvAhW7yDLU

Benzinga, W2AV Talk™ Exposes the Formula of Better Living, Lifestyle Upgrades, and Enjoying Life
https://www.benzinga.com/pressreleases/21/10/n23684061/w2av-talk-exposes-the-formula-of-better-living-lifestyle-upgrades-and-enjoying-life

Women of More Magazine
https://issuu.com/womenofmoremagazine/docs/wommag_fall_edition_19 (Pages 20-21)

Brighter Days Ahead

ABC (WBRC Breaking News)
https://www.wbrc.com/video/2020/09/22/tips-gaining-financial-independence/

YouTube Show Host: W²AVTalk Opener of W2AV Opener of W2AV Talk with Demetris Curry - YouTube

YouTube Channel ~ https://www.youtube.com/demetriscurry

Thank You

I hope you enjoyed reading and journaling with *Brighter Days Ahead*.
I would love to hear your experience using this book.

Connect with Us
Demetris Curry Online